HOW TO LIVE YOUR LIFE WITHOUT STRESS

It's best to stay present and let go of worry

Douglas Susan

CONTENTS

CHAPTER TWO

BEST PRACTICES FOR LIVING IN THE MOMENT AND STOPPING WORRY

CHAPTER THREE

WHY DO INDIVIDUALS WORRY?

CHAPTER FOUR

INTRODUCTION

Why do people fret over things they can't control? Why do people worry at all? You can discover solutions to these and other questions in this book. You know full well that things aren't always simple or happy in life. Therefore, expressing worry about the issues when life hits you hard makes sense. Overanalyzing, fretting, and feeling the world implode on you are not natural. It is crucial to keep in mind that every individual has a distinct viewpoint and background. Problems are not meant to drag you down but to help you become a better and stronger person. As a result of your experiences, you grow wiser, since wallowing in your suffering will only make you weaker. You can learn how to quit worrying and start living by reading this book.

CHAPTER ONE

TYPES OF WORRY AND THEIR EFFECTS

What Results From Your Worry?

Everyone occasionally worries about something, but some worry more frequently than others, including little matters. These people are said to have a mental disorder known as generalized anxiety disorder (GAD), characterized by continual concerns, anxiety, and worry over even the most minor things, including their jobs, homes, finances, futures, etc.

Generalized Anxiety Disorder: What Is It?

Anxiety disorders are a group of illnesses that include generalized anxiety disorder. Despite your efforts, you have trouble controlling your concerns, anxiety, or worry.

Facts About Worry And The Technique For Analyzing Worry

You frequently lack focus because you are anxious and think about numerous things simultaneously.

Lack of restful sleep and mental peace make having a restful night's sleep challenging, as is finding peace of mind when the mind is agitated and overloaded with thoughts.

Feeling occasionally worn out by life as well as by nothing. Most of the time, you want to give up and have no drive to do anything.

Your persistent fear prevents you from making decisions or moving forward in your life or job. Another sign of concern or anxiety is constant irritability. You get easily aggravated by even the little things.

You experience restlessness, which makes you always moody.

For most people, stress, panic episodes, and emotional trauma can all raise blood pressure to the point where it can be fatal.

Making wise decisions becomes challenging, and you always feel worn out.

Constantly living in fear and worrying about the future.

Worrying can negatively impact your health and potentially result in significant medical problems.

As you'll learn in this book, finding techniques to help you quit overthinking and worrying can help you stay sane and have a healthier and happier life. You'll know how to stop worrying and start living in the moment.

There can be instances where you begin to worry. Remember that worry and concern are two very different things. When people express concern, they are probably trying to develop the most effective remedy for the issue, doing their best to remain open-minded about the outcome.

Worriers consider their current issue while also trying to foresee the outcome of the scenario. They frequently reflect on the outcomes they have previously encountered and things that are not yet real.

Information on Worry and an Analysis Method
You have difficulties because you are a person, which is natural given that neither the world nor people are perfect for developing the most effective remedy for some more prominent

obstacles, making them worry more about whether their predicament is justified.

It is not desirable and is not a good enough justification for excessive thought or worry. Let's examine a few of the root causes of this. People get anxious or worried.

The Causes Of Anxiety And Overthinking

You should be aware that anyone can become anxious over anything. Some people enjoy life and live in the now, which is an excellent strategy for reducing anxiety. Others worry about various issues due to their stress, their family's history, stressful events they are currently going through, or other personal factors. For instance, kids or even adults who are perfectionists or timid and easily influenced frequently experience anxiety, sometimes even at a young age.

Other Types Of Anxiety (Worry)

Other illnesses might develop due to anxiety or concern, in addition to Generalized Anxiety Disorder (GAD). However, you should seek assistance or professional guidance when you realize you cannot manage these circumstances alone.

Take your time with problems; ask for help if necessary. While talking to someone may take time to solve your issue, it is frequently a good place to start when looking for answers. True, the proverb "A problem shared is a problem halved" applies here.

Now let's examine several other anxiety disorders, such as:

Social Anxiety

Anyone or everyone will always experience anxiety or nervousness before performing socially or when they are in various social circumstances that place them in the spotlight.

It could be giving a speech in public, making their high-profile debut at an event, giving a presentation at work or even in school, etc. Even for individuals who participate in these activities frequently, they can make anyone anxious.

You are constantly concerned with how you will come across in front of others and what will happen if you do poorly. Most often, people with poor self-esteem or low self-confidence will develop a fear of being mocked, criticized, ashamed, and other negative emotions.

How to Recognize If You Have Social Phobia

Let's say you are going through one of the symptoms listed below. Consequently, it could be helpful to know:

- Aversion to speaking in public.
- Engaging in social activities.
- Performing other public tasks.
- Anytime you consider such occasions or functions, you start to sweat.
- You quiver and get unsteady, and you may even lack self-confidence.
- When you try to speak or address people, you either compulsively blush or stutter and stumble over your words.
- The final sign that you can see is that you keep needing to use the restroom due to abrupt diarrhea.

You might notice all or some of these symptoms, but scarcely anyone else does.

Many individuals with Social Anxiety Disorder are afraid of talking or doing inappropriate things, especially in front of others, for fear that it will make them look bad or disgrace them.

They would prefer to avoid attending a public event or activity, and if they do, you will notice how cautious they are with their behavior and actions.

It's simple to provide advice and support once you consider why some people have severe social anxiety while others don't.

What Causes Social Phobia?

Some will assert that no one is born with a particular phobia and that it stems from dread of encounters and experiences. Some phobias, though, are inherited and run in the family.

As a result, even though your parents might have difficulty appearing in public, you, as a youngster, will likely share your anxiety and find yourself avoiding social events as you age. The child may get the same phobia as the parent if this is not controlled when they are young.

Another possibility is temperament. It comes naturally to you because of who you are, in which case it can be challenging to exert control once you are an adult.

Based on direct or indirect experience Kids' early development is crucial. Changing the traits you instill in early childhood may be challenging, especially if they are negative ones.

A child's confidence can be damaged by being publicly embarrassed, humiliated, or treated poorly, which can cause them to avoid engaging in numerous social activities.

Children may suffer significant mental and emotional harm if they recall how they were shamed or humiliated when they attempted to respond to a question in class or made a mistake while giving a speech in front of the class.

A Quick Fix For Overcoming Social Phobia
There isn't a rapid cure for this kind of phobia. It is best managed throughout a child's formative years before they grow older or become adults. Seeking advice or expert assistance is an additional option.

Psychological therapy and subsequently, in some circumstances, pharmaceuticals and medications may also become an alternative, the two sorts of treatments that are typically suggested for this fear.

Individual Or Particular Phobia

You may also fall into this group if you have other particular or private fears. Although you might not be afraid of giving speeches in front of large crowds, you may be terrified of heights, animals, flying, or sailing, and this fear will always be present because you have seen people die from some of these things.

People with a personal or specialized phobia frequently overestimate what they perceive as dangerous to their safety or life. These unfounded anxieties result from your emotions or previous contacts and experiences.

<u>An illustration of a specific phobia is:</u>
Fear of animals. This group includes those who are afraid of specific creatures or insects.

Fear of the environment or nature.

Fear of heights, thunder, lightning, water, fire, etc., is an example of this phobia.

Medical anxiety. Some people fall into this group because they fear blood, injections, damage, medications, etc.

There may be more individual phobias that weren't included here. Additionally, as was already established, these phobias are subjective because they are limited to your thoughts, experiences, and perceptions. It might occur due to a childhood encounter that left you fearing it.

Symptoms And Indicators Of A Particular Phobia

Increased excessive and ongoing fear of a specific animal or object.

You start being picky about the people and locations you go to.

In most situations, you avoid meeting new people or going there in general, especially if the thing or animal you're afraid of is nearby.

Most of the time, you can imagine being impacted by these creatures or things for up to a year.

What Leads To Particular Phobias

Like social phobia, this phobia can also be brought on by temperament. You might not like cats or dogs just because it's in your nature for one reason or another.

The individual's family history may also contribute to this form of phobia. If this ailment runs in the family and one or both of your parents or other relatives have it, you'll probably notice the symptoms.

If a dog or a snake has previously bitten you, you may suddenly develop a severe fear of dogs. Additionally, your encounter has caused a phobia for you.

Obsessive-Compulsive Disorder (OCD)

As you were getting ready for work, eating breakfast, and getting into your car one morning, let's say you had an epiphany. You rush back or ask someone to help you check, only to discover that you turned the oven or gas cylinder off that morning.

You still needed to turn it off. According to the example, this nervous thought can occasionally benefit your safety. It is a positive thing since it can save lives.

When these kinds of thoughts occur practically constantly, it develops into OCD. You start to go crazy, which could happen more than once, so you must keep checking the gas and oven; in certain circumstances, you might check them continuously throughout the day.

People who have this kind of disease are frequently ashamed of it. Therefore, they make an effort to keep it a secret from others. Detecting or identifying them when they hide such a condition is incredibly challenging.

The victim starts skipping essential activities as a result, which is when this type of disease is typically discovered.

OCD Symptoms and Signs

Some people may have a filthy obsession and strive to avoid getting their hands dirty. They may also develop a washing obsession because they think anything in the house may be contaminated. Sexual difficulties are a worry for some OCD disorders. The mere mention of sex or other sexual activity makes you feel nauseated.

For many people, having a security phobia results in constant anxiety about their safety and the conviction that someone is stalking them or others they care about.

Nearly everyone on earth adheres to one or more religions since, in our culture, religion is a way of life. However, some people need to pray frequently, believing that something negative might happen if they don't.

Reasons for OCD

This kind of situation might be triggered by two essential sources, namely biological and experiential or environmental variables.

And occasionally, combining the two can enhance the condition's range of effects.

Neurological problems, for example, are one of the leading biological causes of this disease. Signaling between your brain cells is hampered when your serotonin levels are out of equilibrium. It frequently results in brain abnormalities and may cause obsessive-compulsive disorder.

Behavior-related issues might also contribute to this disease. Destructive behaviours spread because they are more readily acquired, especially among peers.

OCD Causes Post-Trauma Stress Disorder

Most people develop negative behaviours or fears after experiencing a traumatic event, disastrous catastrophe, or other situations that might have threatened their lives or safety.
While some people overcome their fear and grow stronger over time, others are traumatized by the prospect of it and typically remain so.

 Losing a family member or other loved one, being in a severe vehicle accident, being the victim of rape or sexual assault, being subjected to torture or abuse, being the victim of fire, and other similar situations can result in post-traumatic stress disorder.

Research has revealed that not everyone can overcome this disease on their own. Therefore, those who experience it should seek quick expert assistance.

Associated Symptoms and Signs of This Condition

In addition to the fact that you might continually see images or memories of prior incidents playing back in your head, you frequently experience fear or panic with even the slightest idea or memory of such an incident.

Most of the time, it seems like you are continually going through the trauma of the past. As a result, you frequently experience nightmares or perhaps flashbacks to the incident.

You don't get enough sleep. After all, you can't relax because you worry that you could be in danger or assaulted at any moment. You are constantly on high alert.

You start to avoid situations or people that can remind you of the occurrence because its effects are so severe. If you were sexually assaulted, you might notice that you started to fear men or even sex.

You exhibit the emotion of unconcern, lose interest in everything, even life, and quit being.

People with this illness are frequently depressed and pallid and develop drug and alcohol addictions, among other symptoms, to lessen the impact of the trauma.

Fear Disorder

When you suffer from panic attacks, you frequently experience abrupt bursts of fear.

You typically have a seizure when images start playing in your head or when you see anything that reminds you of a former gruesome experience or an unpleasant memory from accidents or other causes.

While some people get panic attacks due to their family history or genetics, others experience them as a medical condition; they must be addressed to prevent lasting harm.

Whenever they happen, panic attacks typically last between 10 and 30 minutes. And during that time, you experience fatigue, weakness, and occasionally even worse feelings. This feeling occurs repeatedly every time and may last the entirety of the day.

Signs And Symptoms Predicting A Panic Attack?

Almost everyone who experiences life's highs and lows has or will ultimately have a panic episode. You will typically notice the following symptoms:

Certain situations are more severe than others, and some impact others more.

The sensation of extreme fear or panic, the feeling that you are about to pass out, choke, lose control, or lose your mind

Your heart rate would noticeably elevate.

You start having trouble breathing and think you're running out of air.

I feel choked, excessively sweating, faint, light-headed, or dizzy.

Panic attacks can happen to everyone; there are no age or time constraints.

However, adults are the ones who experience it the most frequently; children and older people are less likely to share it.

Why do panic attacks occur?

An incident of panic isn't usually caused by one specific thing. This condition has several contributing causes.

It could be an illness you have or a genetic problem, and most of the time, it's because of terrible experiences in the past.

Conditions like cardiac arrhythmias, hyperthyroidism, asthma, chronic obstructive pulmonary disease, and irritable bowel syndrome can also bring on panic disorder.

The majority of people only acquire these ailments from their parents. The child might begin exhibiting some of the symptoms if their parents had a severe panic disorder in the past.

When you experience a gruesome situation and have flashes of those moments repeatedly, that is another component that can spread this disease. Seeking a doctor when you have even the slightest symptom is recommended.

If panic attacks are not properly managed, they can cause significant mental illnesses and make you pose a threat to both you and the people around you.

34

HOW TO LIVE YOUR LIFE WITHOUT STRESS

35

CHAPTER TWO

**BEST PRACTICES FOR LIVING IN THE MOMENT
AND STOPPING WORRYING**

How Can Worry Be Best Analyzed?

Look at some troubling facts first; they might make you feel better about the issue. When you consider what is causing you to worry, feel nervous, or feel afraid, your thoughts should wander to someone else who has gone through a similar circumstance (there may be some differences, but they are all basically the same) and emerge stronger.

In other words, there is always a means to overcome a struggle in life, and someone else already has. You must speak with them and stop going through life alone and in silence.

Focus more on the present because it is something you can influence, rather than worrying about what will happen in the future. The effects of stressing or overthinking on your health are something else to keep in mind.

Many individuals are unaware of the adverse effects of excessive worry or anxiety on their health. The study also revealed that some people experience high blood pressure (HBP), which can be brought on by excessive worry and, in the worst situations, can even be fatal.

<u>Asking yourself the following questions can help you when experiencing difficulty, fear, or other</u>

situations that make you feel worried or
uncomfortable:

1. What exactly is the issue, and what would be
the worst-case scenario if there was no workable
solution?

2. What are the underlying reasons of the issue?
Then try to imagine what might happen so that
you are mentally ready for it.

3. What are the potential remedies, and where can
you get further treatments to help you better your
worst-predicted outcomes?

4. What is the best course of action
choosing the best option and seeking guidance
from those who have successfully navigated
similar circumstances?

The Worst Mental Habits You Need To Break

- Worrying is terrible, but it becomes more hazardous when you start thinking negatively about your circumstances.

- Even in the worst cases, a positive outlook may keep you happy and rational. It is crucial to avoid using extreme answers, such as all-or-nothing approaches, whenever you are faced with a challenging issue.

- First, even when it offers solutions, that thinking will worsen the situation and is not necessarily the best option.

- Making snap judgments or poor decisions in response to a circumstance might happen when you arrive at or jump to a hasty conclusion.

- Even the most dire of situations require you to gather your information and consider it carefully before making a decision. This will assist you in coming up with a better answer.

The following elements that will likely impact how you respond to your anxieties are your emotions

When something terrible happens, you get worried or afraid; when you're at ease, you get excited; when you've done something dreadful, you feel guilty; when you're irritated, you get furious; and so on.

These are some of the feelings that humans experience. It is crucial to understand yourself, how to control your emotions, and how people generally worry and become terrified when they are in danger or have problems.

When you have endured trauma or a nasty incident, one thing you experience as a human is doubt. You begin to doubt yourself and perhaps even accuse yourself of putting yourself in an uncontrollable scenario.

 Self-doubt is a severe problem that everyone might encounter. It's been said that if life knocks you down nine times, you get back up ten, but if you doubt your ability, you don't even get back up once.

Setting expectations and goals for oneself is excellent because it helps you develop personally. However, setting improbable standards for yourself will cost you more than it will gain you. When you try to accomplish a lot in a short time, keep in mind that you could also lose a lot in a short amount of time.

 Keep an open mind and try not to get too disappointed, irritated, angry, or lose faith in fate when things don't turn out as you had intended because big expectations come with big rewards and risks.

Everything in life is a coin flip. Thus, your future is up to luck or fate and not something you can control. Everyone needs to understand that every choice involves a chance at life.

You still have to make those decisions, whether they work or not. Accepting this reality makes it simpler to quit blaming yourself for every issue you encounter and to start seeking workable solutions and escape routes.

Control what you can, try your best to make the best decisions, and hope for the best for the things you can't. Even amid challenging circumstances, you will find tranquility through this straightforward exercise.

15 Strategies For Being Present And Stop Worry

1. It would be best if you got past your worries.

2. When faced with problems in life, maintaining your composure and not losing your cool may be pretty gratifying.

3. When you confront a problem, your mind starts to work quickly, presenting many possible outcomes. In every situation, remaining composed will help you comprehend and see things.

4. Instead of worrying about the results, concentrate more on the solutions that would

improve your condition. Make sure you enjoy today as much as you can.

When faced with a challenge, few people can live in the moment. It becomes intimidating when they deal with a more significant issue of self-doubt, typically resulting in bad decisions.

 Nobody ever wants to have issues in life, but since they arise, you can do nothing but deal with them.
The outcomes of the past can also serve as a constant reminder of unpleasant emotions, which many people may attempt to ignore

5. Some people also worry that the future might have the same outcome: People cling to harmful habits like drinking, overeating, using drugs, or having sex to stop the anguish of the past.

The best way to handle such a scenario is to first steer clear of items that frequently bring back bad memories, visualize good recollections from the past, and cultivate an optimistic outlook.

6. Discuss it with someone: Few people enjoy discussing or even sharing their problems with others. They could keep their troubles to themselves since they are uncomfortable talking about them. The issue is that when you endure suffering alone, it consumes you from the inside out until you die or are destroyed.

Only some people are worth opening up to about your difficulties, whether you think they'd take advantage of you or you're the shy type. A professional with a lot of experience can help you solve your problem permanently by listening to your concerns.

7. Be prepared for the worst case scenario: Using this method, you can avoid unrealistic expectations that lead to disappointment. When you have an open mind and recognize that circumstances could go either way, you mentally

prepare for the worst and are less likely to become dissatisfied when things don't work out as you had hoped.

8. Develop mindfulness: Awareness of what is happening is not the only way to live. You stay grounded in reality when you are aware of the moment. When attentive, you have far more control over your thoughts, body, emotions, and environment.

9. Being mindful involves developing awareness of the world and approaching circumstances more calmly and attentively. Simple techniques like meditation and being picky about the actions and activities you participate in can help you build a mindfulness mindset.

10. Use the Stop Loss Technique: The stop loss method is used by stock and forex traders to limit losses before they spiral out of control and forfeit

their investments. You can also take a leaf from this tactic. Cut your losses and go on if you can.

11. Try not to consider what others may say: Do not confuse discussing a matter with a friend, relative, or professional with confiding in a stranger. Choose to whom you relate your experience carefully because not everyone can assist you. Find people who may have experienced similar situations to your own or who may have knowledge that can help you by providing a good solution.

12. Develop the habit of relaxing and calming your nerves: it helps. It helps you relax and think more clearly when you contemplate and rest rather than overthink.

13. Always take a nap; after all, some individuals have it worse off than you do.

14. Put all of your attention on finding solutions. Always question your assumptions and strive to

solve your immediate difficulties with long term answers.

15. Change your negative attitude: Never assume the worst or that anything will go wrong because your instinct tells you it will. You start thinking about "what if the ship sinks" and other unfavorable scenarios when you want to see the ocean. This thinking will instill dread and doubt in you and skew your judgment.

Ten Things That Are Not Worth Your Time To Worry About

1. How to Pay the Bills: Don't let worrying about your bills keep you awake at night because they will always be there. Take things one step at a time, work hard, and do your best.

2. Making money: Everyone wants to make good money since it provides comfort. But resist allowing it to dominate your thinking.

3. Forget Your Past: Your past shouldn't serve as punishment; it should serve as a guide.

4. What will people say? Because everyone always has something to say, worrying about what everyone will say could drive you nuts. As it is your life and your only one, do what is best for you.

5. You want to leave the house today, but you are concerned about the traffic, the possibility that your car may break down, etc. You always worry about things going wrong, which carries a negative attitude and influences your judgments and decisions.

6. Your occupation or employment: Work stress may be highly upsetting and draining, mainly if you are outside your ideal profession. If your job

doesn't make you happy, leave and find something that does.

7. Aging is a normal part of life; you can't stay young forever. You must acknowledge these truths and be willing to consider them.

8. Everybody passes away eventually and at some point.

9. Being flawless: Since nobody is ideal and the universe contains flaws, why must you make yourself perfect?

10. You Make Mistakes: Mistakes will undoubtedly occur, but don't let them define you. Take the advice you were given and use it to your advantage.

CHAPTER THREE

WHY DO INDIVIDUALS WORRY?

Does Overthinking And Worrying Help?

Everyone experiences worry at some point; what is abnormal is excessive worry and difficulty controlling your anxieties and emotions. Some people are frequently urged to seek professional assistance when their fears get out of control.

Let's use a person who keeps a dog as a pet as an example. In my experience, dogs make the ideal companions for guys. If this dog disappears for whatever reason, it would be almost as devastating as losing a family member, perhaps a brother, and you might start to lose your mind. Eating will also begin to be a problem; you'll start exhibiting indications of restlessness, you'll begin to worry that your dog will get lost, you'll probably start to overthink the situation, and you'll begin to feel quite uncomfortable and disturbed.

If, after a thorough search, you discovered the dog playing with other dogs in a neighbor's garden, you wouldn't need to be concerned.

This straightforward illustration can be adapted to circumstances that might cause anxiety and panic. People overthink everything, allowing trivial issues to bother them or keeping them up all night overthinking.

You'll discover how to quit worrying about life's problems and begin living in this book. Additionally, you will learn some of the consequences of excessive concern and effective strategies for dealing with this illness (excessive worry is a mental habit that can potentially cause serious harm, if not death).

When attempting to address why individuals worry, it is essential first to recognize that worrying or anxiety entails incorrect thinking and that even the circumstances you worry about may or may not occur, leading you to worry about nonexistent issues.

Furthermore, even if it does happen and you are powerless to prevent it, it is nonetheless common in life. Therefore, there is no need to commit suicide over issues mainly out of your control. Although worrying is inevitable, there are ways to manage it.

So many people will tell you to direct your energy towards the present moment rather than fretting about what's to come. The present moment. Here and now. This adage doesn't state that you shouldn't create plans; on the contrary, humans are the only species capable of doing so. However, sometimes those plans don't turn out as we had hoped. That's life; you win and lose some.

The Causes Of Worry And Overthinking

People frequently worry (or experience anxiety) when they anticipate significant events, are under stress from challenging circumstances, or, for some, while worrying about unimportant things or asks other suspicious inquiries that occasionally give you the creeps, you might already have generalized anxiety disorder. However, worrying is almost normal when it does not always happen.

Only an expert can give sound advice on this subject or in any medical field dealing with this condition. To assist with managing and addressing this issue, people with overthinking or worrying disorders are frequently encouraged to seek professional assistance. If you worry excessively, you might experience physical symptoms, including headaches, nausea, exhaustion, irregular heartbeats, tight muscles, etc.

CHAPTER FOUR

MEDITATION TO EASE YOUR WORRY

Stop Stressing By Practicing Mindfulness And Contemplation

While stressing, you'll have a difficult time centering on anything else. However, consistent rumination on negative thoughts could be a bad habit.

When you feel your concentration melting away, sitting in a calm room and clearing your mind can do wonders for your well-being. Mindfulness and reflection can take your focus away from negative thoughts, prevent you from feeling anxious, and inspire a state of calm.

A Guided Meditation App

It can assist you in de-stressing, helping you to concentrate your thoughts, or clearing your head.Over time, meditation can also help you get into a flow state, allowing you to focus on your needs and tackle tasks on your to-do list with ease. Learning to focus on what's before you, rather than your worries, can truly change your life.

Practicing Deep Breathing

When we stress, we often focus on negative things that might happen in the future. Staying in the present moment can help soothe worries and negative thinking and also reduce physical symptoms.

When you become anxious, you could have trouble breathing or feel pain in your chest. Practicing deep breathing can divert your attention from your worries and help you become grounded in the present.

Whether you're having trouble sleeping or you feel a panic attack coming on, deep breathing is a quick and easy way to stop stressing.

Doing A Body Check

When you're stressing, it's natural to tense your muscles. Over time, lifted shoulders or a tight jaw can lead to persistent muscle strain. The more you stress, the more tension you continuously carry in your body. If you feel constant tension, stiffness, or pain in your back and shoulders, it's time to focus on how to stop stressing.

In these moments, as you notice yourself feeling stressed, take a deep breath and note where you're feeling pressure. Scanning your body can help you reconnect to the present, feel more grounded, and ultimately stress less.

Begin at your toes and pay devoted attention to each part of your body up to your head. When you feel tension, Focus on physically relaxing and breathing into any discomfort you experience when you feel tense. Slowly release the tightness in your body, and before you know it, you'll have found one effective method for how to stop worrying instantly.

Stop Stressing By Focusing On What You're Grateful For

As we focus on one negative thought, it primes our brain to seek more. In contrast, looking for a silver lining can help train your brain to seek positives and break the cycle of stress. This is one of the many benefits and potentially life-changing possibilities of establishing a regular thankfulness practice.

Having trouble finding something to be thankful for? Take a step back and look for what is interesting about the situation or humorous. Engage your mind through curiosity and humor. This can quickly shift you into a better place and provide a necessary break from the negative thoughts. You can even try to be curious about the way you stress.

While it may take practice, learning to turn your negative thoughts around can be an excellent way to stop stressing.

Keeping A Daily Emotions Diary

Chronic stress and anxiety occur when we don't notice the initial signs of stress and let it build over time. Want to learn how to stop worrying? Checking in with yourself regularly is an essential way to preserve your mental well being and manage your anxiety.

By the time we're in a stress cycle, we often feel disconnected from our emotions. Keeping a daily diary can help you track patterns and effectively manage stress before your feelings spiral out of control.

As you practice journaling your emotions and sharing your thoughts, it becomes easier to recognize when you're starting to worry. Stopping stress early will ultimately help you feel better and stay focused on what matters most to you.

Maintaining A Regular Sleep Schedule

Insomnia is a common symptom of chronic stress. When your mind is racing, it can be challenging to relax and get enough sleep. While you may feel like staying up will help you "solve" your stresses, you're often better off with a restful night's sleep.

Without rest, minor worries can trigger a stress response that persists for days or weeks in a cycle of stress.

Here's how to stop stressing and finally get some rest:

Before going to bed, practice some mindfulness or meditation.

Just before going to bed, read a book or sip a cup of soothing tea.

Stop using devices at least an hour before bedtime (social media is shown to be linked to anxiety).

Make use of organic sleep aids like essential oils, melatonin, and lavender.

If you find it difficult to stop thinking, try journaling for a little while (just give yourself a time limit so you can still get to bed on time!).

You deserve to stop stressing and take back control of your life, so never hesitate to ask for help when you need it.

Make a distinction between the things you can and cannot control.

Stressing is typically focused on a problem that needs to be controlled, putting our focus on "what if" rather than the present moment.

Many people mistakenly believe that spending more time worrying about a problem will make it easier to find a solution.

If you find it difficult to stop worrying all the time, ask yourself, "What can I control? This will help you become more self-reliant when it comes to taking action. Moreover, this mindset can help release your stress when you find there's nothing you need to do about the situation.

CONCLUSION

When life knocks you down hard, remember that it can only break you if you allow it. It would help if you fought back physically, mentally, and in other ways. Embrace a never-say-die attitude and remember that nothing in life is worth your life.

Always attempt to reach out when you are going through a difficult time, and never suffer alone. As the phrase goes, "A problem shared is a problem solved." Always return to pleasant memories to lessen the pain and bring you peace.

Find something that will make you happy or do anything to divert your attention from evil thoughts. It is normal to feel worried when anything is going wrong or you are having a problem. However, when you start to worry and fear, things get worse, since that's when you begin to make poor decisions.
Even in the face of peril, maintain your composure; it will soothe your nerves and clarify your mind. Use the past as a lesson, but never dwell on it; take what you've learned and move on. Life is too short.